GEAR BEAR ADVENTURES

GEAR BEAR ADVENTURES

AS TOLD BY GEAR BEAR

L. A. SYMONS

iUniverse LLC
Bloomington

GEAR BEAR ADVENTURES
As Told by Gear Bear

iUniverse books may be ordered through booksellers or by contacting:

iUniverse LLC
1663 Liberty Drive
Bloomington, IN 47403
www.iuniverse.com
1-800-Authors (1-800-288-4677)

ISBN: 978-1-4917-0186-7 (sc)
ISBN: 978-1-4917-0187-4 (hc)
ISBN: 978-1-4917-0188-1 (ebk)

Library of Congress Control Number: 2013913899

Printed in the United States of America

iUniverse rev. date: 08/28/2013

Contents

Follow the mighty adventures of a small
but powerful brown bear
named Gear Bear.

To my family and friends for putting up with me as I hauled Gear Bear everywhere we have been for the past twenty-one years and neither complaining nor telling me I was insane. I am sure they thought it though!

Acknowledgments

I would like to thank all the people who have treated Gear Bear as one of the family.

In addition, I would like to thank the store owners, security personnel, the US Marshal Service, Oklahoma state troopers, the Tunica, Mississippi Sheriff's Department, American Airlines, tour guides, the folks at Cross Country Trail Ride, and everyone who took the time to have a photo or two taken with Gear Bear and share their stories with me.

But most of all, thank you to my loving family and to everyone who has met Gear Bear, thanks for having such great sense of humor!

Prologue

Let me introduce myself. I am a small brown bear that has had the pleasurable opportunity to travel just about everywhere my friends and family have gone. (That is if they didn't leave me behind, forget me, or lose me.)

Because I am always ready for a new adventure, I have even had the chance to travel with my family's friends and share their adventures or, more often than not, their misadventures.

I hope you enjoy reading my stories as much as I enjoy telling them.

I'll Start at the Beginning, 1992

The earliest memory I have as a young bear cub is being unwrapped from white tissue paper while being flown on a big airplane to an unknown destination. As the tissue was slowly removed, I looked up and saw a pair of bright blue eyes staring back into my little brown peeps.

To tell you the truth, the attention scared the heck out of me. Had I been bear-napped? Bought on the black market? I did not know, but as everything turned out, I was about to start a wonderful, adventurous life with a very loving family: Paula, the blue-eyed matriarch, and the rest of her clan.

In order to understand how I became a constant traveling companion, it might be best if I told you about a friend of mine, Flat Stanley. In case you have not heard of him, Flat Stanley is a character in a book written by Jeff Brown in 1964. The story involves Stanley and his brother, Arthur, and tells us how Stanley became flat. Because of his skinniness, Stanley is able to travel the world by way of an envelope and a postage stamp.

In 1994, schools began a Flat Stanley project that allowed children in primary grades to create and send a paper version of Stanley to friends and relatives around the world. When their Flat Stanleys returned, the children wrote stories about his adventures.

I'm not as tall as my friend Stan. But, if I stand on my tippy toes, I might be able to reach the nine-inch mark on a ruler. I'm also not nearly as skinny as Flat Stanley. This means I have to travel by more conventional methods than through the mail. And travel I have!

Thanks to Paula and her family and friends for taking me wherever they go, I have many miles under my belt, a lot of stamps on my passport, and countless stories to tell. I hope you enjoy these stories of my adventures, photos, and the friends I have met along the way.

This is me at the beginning!

Background Check

Because the memory of emerging from wrapping paper did not really take me back to my true beginnings, I thought, *Bear, you should do some research on yourself to find out where you're from.*

Well, I found out I was born in 1986 in Edison, New Jersey. My birth name is Kinder, but friends call me Gear Bear. (In case you are wondering how to pronounce my first name, "Gear" rhymes with "Bear".)

I learned in my search that I have a cousin! So I decided to use some of my free time to search of him or maybe her. That led to visiting courthouses, libraries, and hospitals, so if you're interested in hearing about that, please venture along on my journey.

"Adopt" means to assume responsibility for and rear a child (or bear cub) of other parents as one's own child. It also means to take or receive into any kind of new relationship; to adopt a cub as a protégé

I like the word protégé because I believe that is exactly what Paula and her family think I am—Paula's protégé. They have been taking care of me for many years now—always confirming I have my suitcase packed and my teeth brushed, and they make sure I have clean underwear on and that I say my prayers.

Thanks to Paula and her family, I am always warm, usually dry (you will read about my water exploits) and well fed. Life is good!

Because I know the Gear Bear Family does not stop or start with me, I am very, very interested in searching for my "other" family members.

Let's see how that works out for me!

You Won't Get Wet—We Promise!

Water exploits—let me begin my adventures there. Being so leery of water—I even shower with a snorkel and mask—it took a lot of convincing to get me to agree to an excursion on the Wisconsin River.

It was Saturday morning, and a group of us were sitting on the banks of the river waiting for our turn to launch our loaded canoes. The first sign that this might not be the canoe float I expected occurred when I got wet getting onto the canoe. Notice I did not say *into* the canoe. That is correct; I was duct taped to the front of the canoe with a baggie serving as a raincoat. I told myself that if I got out of this alive, I would never put myself in such danger again. Wrong.

Because I was chosen as navigator of the fleet, I took my job seriously. As we floated down the river, I continually kept a lookout. During a routine right-to-left glance, I quickly snapped back to the right. *Oh my gosh!* We were floating through the nudist part of the Wisconsin River called Blue Moon. Remember the part of the song, "Ethyl don't look"? Tell you what, I done looked, and I sure wish I hadn't.

Never in my life have I considered what old men and women look like naked, but there they were, strolling down the riverbank and scarring me for life. As hard as I tried, I couldn't get the image out of my head. I had no idea why this group of California raisins was as proud as a flock of peacocks strutting their stuff. It sure looked like they had been baked in the sun way too long.

Overall, the float trip was exciting and enjoyable except for the part when they removed duct tape from my little sunburned body. The chances of hair growing in my new bald spots are about as likely as me forgetting what I saw as I canoed down the Wisconsin River.

Family Night

I, Gear Bear, could very well be a great ambassador for families!

Because I have no clue where I came from or who my 'real' mother is, I believe Paula has really started a fantastic tradition. If it's Wednesday, it is *family night*! Just ask any of the little ones in our clan.

There is one rule of family night: If you can make it, that's great. So far three out of four families have made it every week. What happened to the fourth family? Well, that is the reason we had Mexican night! You see, Lyn and little Karlos are presently still in Mexico, awaiting a visa to bring the little guy home so they, too, can enjoy our family nights together. It has been more than five years since Lyn went to Mexico to adopt her little guy. She has not been back to the United States since. We hope they hurry home to all of us; I bet Paula will let them cook on the next Mexican night!

On our last Mexican night, the main course was tacos. Leigh did an exceptional job of dicing, chopping, and preparing the meat and all the extras. The meal was served buffet style, so I put as much stuff in my taco as I wanted, which was a lot because I thought the tortilla was bigger than I was. The meal was rather messy, but I managed to eat the whole thing *and* save enough room for dessert. I'm glad I did because Jean made delicious apple enchiladas, served with a little whipped cream on top. I threw in a cold glass of milk to drink, and it was awesome!

As you can see, I was the center of attention *again*! Well actually, I was the "centerpiece."

In the picture, I am the short one (in case you haven't figured it out) wearing the Cozumel T-shirt and my favorite sombrero.

Oh! The other fellow is young Karlos. He's also wearing his favorite hat while he's in Mexico. I believe we are going to have so much fun when he comes home.

I'm looking forward to next week; the guys are cooking, and it'll be a Halloween-themed family night. Since we are carving the pumpkins *after* dinner, we shouldn't have to worry about finding fingers in the goulash.

In My Opinion

After spending a week in Central Florida visiting several Disney parks, this entry is being written on a plane as I fly back to my home state of Illinois. After putting up such a fuss about being stuck in the baggage compartment, I now fly first class all the way. Although my surroundings are plush and my traveling companions are near me, I cannot help saying I am looking forward to being home again.

Mr. Walt Disney had a wonderful idea to develop entertaining theme parks for people of all ages. But, man, have things gotten out of hand with the crowds. There are approximately 46,500 guests visiting Disney parks each day, but the count can, and does, go up to as high as 100,000 visitors per day, depending on the time of the year. Because it seems I'm always going on one of those really busy days, I told myself the last time I went to Disney World would be my last time, and I'm vowing the same thing again. "Goodbye, Disney World; I hope to never return."

When an amusement park offers valet parking for baby strollers, that's a sign there are way too many people. We left a stroller at the entrance of a ride, and when we returned to it after the ride, we found it was gone. We knew exactly where we'd parked it, but it wasn't there because a park employee wheeled it away and placed it in a stroller parking lot somewhere near the ride. So we began the hunt, using the bags left in the stroller to identify the correct buggy.

I'm not sure, but in my opinion, Disney management should set an age restriction for parks. *No* child under the age of six or any adult over the age of fifty-five should be permitted. That, my friends, would save a lot of crying in both age brackets, *and* it would eliminate the need for that darn stroller parking!

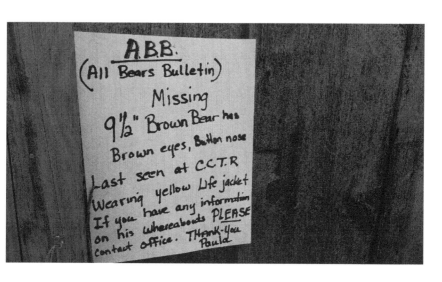

All Bears Bulletin

Whoever thought one would have to wear a lifejacket while horseback riding?

Once or twice a month from May through November, the small town of Eminence, Missouri, which has a population of three hundred people, hosts an awesome seven-day trail ride. Our plan this year was to attend one of the rides.

Now, I was not too keen on this horse thing, but Paula always made sure I was secure on her saddle, even if it meant tying me onto a D-hook with a zip tie. Sometimes she put me into her cup holder and fastened me with a tie.

As you may remember, I do not do water well, so Paula was kind enough to put a bright yellow lifejacket on me before our daily ride up into the town of Eminence. On this particular morning I was tied in extra tight because we were going to cross the Jack Fork River, and neither one of us wanted to take any chances. With the lifejacket on and the zip tie tied, I was ready to hit the road. Our first stop was the top of the hill. Paula dismounted and went into the store. She reappeared ten minutes later, but I was gone. I must have been knocked senseless because I don't remember a thing. Did I fall off the horse? Did I even reach the top of the hill? Where was I? I was now classified as a "missing bear."

Paula retraced her steps all the way back to camp. She looked in every place imaginable. Without any luck of finding me, she sought the help of an expert. It just so happens that one of the riders Paula rode with the day before was a Texas marshal. He had retired a few years earlier, but he was still active in the security of a courthouse.

Taking Marshal Smith's advice, Paula waited twenty-four hours before posting an all bears bulletin (ABB) on me. I was told it was like an APB, but being a bear and all, I could see the difference. I was now a wanted bear, with posters hanging throughout the campgrounds. My likeness adorned the main gate, the arena, and even the dining hall walls. At least I wasn't up on the post office walls.

Within twenty minutes, I had been found! It seemed that someone going through the chow line saw the ABB at the cashier's desk and returned me to Carolyn in the main office. Carolyn immediately announced the great news over the intercom for all to hear.

Following the investigation, it appeared I must have been tied with a faulty zip tie and had fallen off the horse early that morning, right outside of camp.

Carolyn said my bright yellow lifejacket was what caught the eye of the rider and got her to dismount and pick me up. My rescuer mentioned seeing me the day before, riding with Paula, and knew I must have been someone pretty darn important.

Paula and I were just glad that someone took the time to pick me up from the road and not just pass me by or leave me for dead because we're all important in our own ways. Besides that, how would Paula have explained this one to her family?

Buckaroos

Buckaroo boots and short shorts? This was just not right! We had been sitting and enjoying our morning coffee at the Blue and White Café outside of Tunica. If you are from Mississippi, you know exactly what and where I am talking about. In case you are unaware of the Blue and White, it is probably one of the best cafés in the south. Established in 1924, the restaurant was originally owned and operated by the Pure Oil Company.

The story began one Sunday morning when the diner was not yet very busy. A few of the locals and a couple of uniformed good ol' boys were having their morning donut break when it all began. I believe it was when the officers started laughing so hard that I just had to turn around to see what was happening.

The front door opened, and in walked a whole off-kilter family, but the tall, thin man with shoulder-length, gray hair and one-tooth smile really seized my attention. His red buckaroos and cutoff short shorts (the pockets extended beyond the shorts) just stopped me in my tracks. Talk about a vision to behold! This was one that made it tough to hold my laughter.

I take note that I have never been known to be a fashion expert; however, I am positive, just positive, that nowhere in the Harley dress code is this kind of attire approved. How do I know the fashion nightmare was a Harley rider? He wore a Tie-dyed Harley Davidson T-shirt to complete his outfit.

Needless to say, the man and his clothing made me ashamed to admit I was a biker bear.

Little Children and Da Bear

So what could possibly be better than being dragged around by one's ear?

Nothing! Nothing at all.

I am such a lucky bear. When I am not traveling the world, one of my favorite things to do is spend time with my special little friends.

Yesterday was all about Elizabeth, one of my newest little friends, and celebrating her first birthday.

There were several little people celebrating with her. Of course the NaNa's and the PaPa's were present and all the cousins and the aunts and uncles. But, my favorite of course was the cake and ice cream and lots and lots of balloons. We would have probably had more balloons, had not a certain adult "Uncle TJ" been sucking helium out of some of the balloons and then when he talked he sounded very, very silly.

I'm not sure what that was all about. I guess it was an adult thing!

Children are so much fun to watch, no matter what age they are.

Graduation Day

People always say, "Getting there is half the fun." Well, we got there, and it was not fun!

Two days ago, I arrived in Denver, Colorado, "half in the bag." One might say. Let me explain. I was packed in a carry-on to save room in the bag that went beneath the seat. Lo and behold, I did not get on board like I'm used to. It seems, if one is flying American Eagle, when one has a carry-on, one may carry it onto the plane but, may not always have room in the overhead compartment to put your bag.

So as Paula stands dumb founded the stewardess was more than happy to take the bag, (which I might add I was in,) back to the front of the plane . . . . boy was I thinking I was going to be riding 1st class. Boy, was I wrong!

Where did I ride? In the cargo area of the plane with the strollers, car seats, and all the other cargo items. What were they thinking? It was cold, dark, and—can you believe this?—I had *no services*!

Following the hassle in the airport, I could have used a tiny bit of pampering. Our departure time changed eleven times. We boarded a plane and waited. We deplaned and waited and then waited some more before the gate changed and I finally got on a new plane, albeit in the cargo area.

I'll share with you, in my next adventure, our day exploring the big city of Denver. Right now, all I need to worry about is how I am going to walk down that aisle at the Merchandise Mart on Saturday afternoon with Leigh, to receive that BS Degree she has worked so hard for. Congratulations!

Denver in December

What an awesome city to visit at Christmastime!

We all gathered at the Denver Merchandise Mart for the well-organized graduation ceremony. Seeing all of those young and not-so-young people receiving their degrees, in a number of different disciplines was very moving. It must have been a hard and long road to graduation, and I was so proud to be a part of the celebration.

We stayed at the very nice Hampton Inn & Suites in downtown Denver. Because we were so close to the city center, the hotel had valet parking, which we had to pay for. The valets were more than helpful in giving directions and visiting with five-year-old Ben, which is important to me. I appreciate when other people react and interact kindly with small people like me!

From our hotel we had a beautiful view of the state capitol building. (The view would have been more beautiful if there had been snow, but unfortunately there wasn't any. The weather was nice though.) We were also close to the United States Mint, the Molly Brown House Museum, and the famous 16th Street Mall, which we could walk to.

One building that Ben noticed on our walk around the city center was the Brown Palace Hotel. I was so surprised by how much a youngster like him knew about the haunted history of the hotel. He told Leigh and me that when the hotel was remodeled, the switchboard in the main lobby began receiving calls from room 904. When employees answered the call, all they heard was static. This was very intriguing because room 904 had been completely gutted and was under renovation at the time, which meant no phone lines were connected. Local legend grew to be that the mysterious caller may have been a heartbroken socialite who once lived in that room from 1940 to 1955.

Ben's grandpa had read the Brown Palace Hotel ghost story to him a year ago, and Ben recalled the story and the hotel as soon as he saw it from across the street.

I am really glad I get to hang around with such a smart kid. He's like a little walking tour guide.

As we took our tour of downtown Denver, we encountered something rather interesting. We ended up right in the middle of Occupy Denver protesters. There were tents and people camping and sitting in lawn chairs. It felt a lot like a KOA.

Our final visit in downtown Denver was to the Denver Aquarium. At this tourist destination, we visited several exhibits, including *The Rainforest, At the Wharf,* and *Under the Sea,* but my favorite event involved the Mystic Mermaids.

As luck would have it, we were seated adjacent to the *Under the Sea* exhibit at lunchtime. When the music started, Ben and I were able to go right up to the glass tank and watch the mermaids swim and play and interact with the fish in their aquarium setting. One of the mermaids even swam directly to Ben and put her hand against the glass, and we connected—the three of us. This was something we will never forget!

On our last day in Colorado, we visited the little town of Georgetown and the ski town of Breckenridge, where we rode the tram up the mountain to the ski resort.

When we reached the slopes, the Dew Tour, which showcases action sports, was in full swing. After watching those young athletes twist, turn, and somersault on snowboards, I'm really glad they don't make those sticks for guys my size. I had enough trouble hanging onto Ben while he was walking on the snow to the starting line of the competition. Ben was slipping and sliding all the way down the hill.

I sure hope he never wants to learn how to ski or snowboard. I can only imagine where I would be riding on those adventures.

Who Gave the Kid a Slingshot?

My former friend, Ben, just got a new toy. Guess what it is, and guess who got the first and *last* ride.

Thank goodness Ben is not very strong. I did not fly too far. I only reached the neighbor's yard, which in itself can be a scary place! Picking myself up, I dusted off my fur, and walked home. Well actually, I ran home because the neighbor's dog thought I was a new chew toy.

I won't add anything else on this subject—a picture is worth a thousand words.

(By the way, I have absolutely no knowledge of what happened to Ben's new toy!)

Da Bear in Omaha

"It's a beautiful day in the neighborhood . . ." Wait! That is what Mr. Rogers always sang.

We were told that if we backseat passengers behaved, we were going to stop at the Omaha Zoo. Because we were angels, the promise was kept. Unfortunately, we had to park all the way in the back of the lot because we had a horse trailer following us very closely; it was, in fact, attached to our bumper. Fortunately, the weather was perfect, so we didn't need our coats.

Our first stop was the ticket booth. Now that was really cool. They told me I didn't need a ticket, which I loved. Sometimes being short isn't all that bad.

Because there are approximately one hundred fifty acres within the walls of the Henry Doorly Zoo and Aquarium, we decided to start our visit by riding the Skyfari across the park. It wasn't too thrilling because visiting the park in the off-season meant our ride was round-trip—no getting off at the other side. However, we did get to see a lot of interesting animals from our vantage point. The Skyfari took us over giraffes, cheetahs, and much, much more. The zoo also included the Wildlife Carousel and a railroad, neither of which were operating at the time of our visit.

What set this zoo apart from others we have visited was the *Bernice Grewcock Butterfly and Insect Pavilion*. As we walked in, we had to go through several sets of doors to actually get to the butterflies. Once inside, we found ourselves enveloped by hundreds of majestic, free-flying butterflies in their tropical environment. Their diversity and colors were overwhelming.

I was pretty sure Ben wasn't all that thrilled with the magnificent butterflies. Even though they were just small creatures flying around, he didn't like them landing on his back or face.

When leaving the pavilion, we had to make sure that we didn't have a winged hitchhiker on our backs or heads. Personally, I was more afraid of being captured and living out my days in a cocoon in this building, but I made it through just fine.

I am not going to talk about the insect part of the *Bernice Grewcock Butterfly and Insect Pavilion* because Ben was in such a hurry to get out of that part of the exhibit, that we didn't have a chance to see any of it. One might think that maybe he doesn't like bugs.

When we exited, I asked Ben if he minded sitting down for a little while since I was pretty exhausted. As you might remember, my little legs have to work four times faster than his.

Well, I got to rest and rest and rest some more. Yep! They forgot me. From what I understand, several minutes passed before Ben asked Paula, "Where's Gear Bear?" Good thing he is a responsible child and came back for me!

The next stop after reuniting was *Hubbard Gorilla Valley*. This was pretty awesome. Gorillas roam free, and the visitors are on display! This incredible exhibit opened in 2004 and cost of $14 million dollars.

After an exhausting walk through the *Desert Dome*, which was our next exhibit, this is where we traveled through southern Africa, Australia's Red Center, and the Sonora Desert of the southwest United States, I was ready to head east toward home. Ben's and my fatigue may or may not have been the reason we passed on the *Kingdoms of the Night* exhibit, which was beneath the desert floor and is the world's largest nocturnal exhibit. They say hundreds of bats can be seen flying around in the bat cave. But our little legs sure did ache but, we had a great time. The Omaha Zoo is a must-see if you ask me!

Born to be Wild!

As I count down the minutes, I am getting so excited. Soon I'll be tying on my dew rag, slipping on my Harley shirt (no, it's not tie-dyed), and singing "Born to be Wild." Yes! It's party time. Bands, babes and bikes! Sturgis here I come!

Wait! Where are you putting me? Something is wrong with this picture. *You want me to ride where*? I thought I had straightened this out when we flew to Denver last December; I ride up front, *not* in the luggage compartment. And this was even worse than the mix-up to Denver. Instead of being inside, I'm holding on for dear life *to* the luggage rack. I was "blowin' in the wind," one might say.

Because of the awesome views, one of my favorite stops is Chamberlain, South Dakota. The little stores in the area also provide a welcome rest—the highlight being the annual visit to Al's Oasis. For several years, Suburban Harley Davidson always furnished the wait-staff with Harley shirts, but the T-shirts have disappeared since a change in ownership.

This past year, Paula met Marsha, one of the ladies who worked at Al's Oasis. Marsha mostly worked part-time during bike week. After exchanging e-mail addresses and talking about those darn T-shirts, or lack thereof, Paula said she was going to see if her local Harley shop would be interested in doing a little advertising and maybe bringing those bike week shirts back out west.

Another town we hit on the way to Sturgis was Wall. Almost as soon as we hit I-90 in South Dakota, if not before, we started seeing Wall Drug signs. Well, I didn't see the signs *because* I was riding backwards, but I just knew they were there. Wall, South Dakota, population 781, is located about sixty miles west of Mount Rushmore. When Wall Drug was purchased back in 1931, it was a 231-person town "in the middle of nowhere." Now five hundred miles' worth of billboards, stretching from Minnesota to Billings, Montana, on I-90 direct you to nowhere. Where else can you still get free ice water and a cup of coffee for five cents?

That ice water was needed because Paula decided to try out a CamelBak hydration pack this year. If you are familiar with this water carrier, you know one has to bite on the end of a tube and then suck to get the water. All I'm going to say is Paula came home with most of the same water she left with. Every time Paula tried to use the darn thing, I'd get rained on, and of course they were hot drops since I was in the back, clinging to the chrome, and the water sitting in the tube was in direct sunlight. *I wonder what great idea this woman is going to come up with next!*

With eighty-three miles to go to reach our destination, we'd be holding up in a local hotel for a few days. If you were hoping for Sturgis stories, sorry! I believe Sturgis is a lot like Vegas. What happens in Sturgis *should stay* in Sturgis. You'll have to make do with my photos. And yes, I'm keeping the good ones for myself.

Planes, Trains, and Automobiles

First we traveled by automobile to reach the bus. Then we traveled by bus to reach the plane. Then we traveled by plane to reach the train. And finally we traveled by train to reach an automobile. What a circle! It was quite the journey, but I had made it and was ready for my new adventure!

I must mention through all these years of traveling by plane that I have met a lot of different people. Some have been very nice, some not so nice. I have met celebrities, athletes, authors, and airplane pilots, but I must mention the not-so-lovely lady who occupied the seat next to mine on my flight.

To begin, the woman was upset because she was sitting in the wrong seat—my seat. As I walked down the aisle, I heard her say, "We'll see if anyone sits here," and I watched her slide one seat over from her traveling companion, who must have been her husband because neither of them spoke more than ten words to each other the entire four hours we were airborne.

Well, Mrs. Lovely—I will call her—plopped back into her seat, 14B, when she realized 14C, my aisle seat, would not be vacant. She became very upset, not necessarily with me, but with the fact she was stuck in the middle seat, right next to her probable husband.

Mrs. Lovely even copped an attitude with the flight attendant. When provided with a beverage, she insisted on putting it on the floor rather than her tray table. Mrs. Lovely practically had to bend in half to open the can, pour the drink into her glass, and store it at her feet. Now, the stewardess asked the woman to please use the tray table, but Mrs. Lovely just glared at her. I exercised restraint while the lady was bending over—and her undies were showing— against grabbing those tighty-whities and yanking just as hard as I could to give her a much-deserved wedgie. Maybe that would have adjusted her attitude.

The woman's traveling companion was almost as bad as she was. He got up three times and squeezed between my tray table and the seat in front of me. In my humble opinion, three times to the restroom and three times back deserved at least one, "Excuse me." Or maybe he might want to consider a pair of Depends the next time he travels—or better yet, request an aisle seat.

Although it was possible this charming pair were both having bad days, I was pretty sure their next flight experience would be much improved if she requested an aisle seat and he watched his liquid intake before boarding. I hoped their return trip to Chicago was better and that we would *not* be on the same flight!

We arrived in fabulous Las Vegas, but we only stayed long enough to pick up a rental car and head to the Western Zion Park Inn and Conference Center in Springdale, Utah.

The drive was a little longer than we had anticipated, and I had fallen fast asleep in the back seat. When we arrived, it was dark and I had no concept of our surroundings. The woman at the front desk was very, very helpful. She gave me a map of the park and set me up in a room on the first floor because there are no elevators at the lodge and my short legs couldn't climb the stairs. Coming down has never been much of a problem; I slide down the railing—although that sudden drop to the floor at the end of the rail gets me every time.

The view out of our window was totally awesome in the morning. As I looked out and saw the red rock formations, it looked just as if someone had put up a backdrop for a movie set. It was mid-November so the weather was getting colder, but our scenic drive through the park was unforgettable. I thought this would be a place one could spend several days exploring and hiking the trails.

Hotel Security Alert

My travel companions should have kept better track of me because it seemed I was always getting lost.

As this particular story unfolded, I was riding in the zipper compartment of Paula's luggage with my little arms and head sticking out—you know, the usual travel arrangements—when we entered the lobby of our Las Vegas hotel. Although we learned our room was not quite ready yet, we were given the key and told we could leave our luggage inside. After getting off the elevator on the fifteenth floor, we noticed housekeeping still had several rooms to finish up in our area, so we set our bags in the closet right inside the door of our room. I was exactly where I was supposed to be *until* . . .

Paula and Teresa continued with their day and registered for their classes that were to start the following morning. When on a business trip, it was understood that I was to stay put. No sightseeing, swimming, shopping, or getting into trouble.

If you can imagine a little guy like myself quietly minding my own business while hanging out of Paula's suitcase, I believe I was a victim of bear-napping just waiting to happen. Kind of like taking candy from a baby—a no-brainer—and sure enough, a little kid walked by and grabbed my little arm, and away I went. The nabbing happened so fast, my head spun. All I could think was, *This isn't looking good. If Paula finds out I left the room, I'm going to be bear meat.*

The kid must have been looking for a swimming partner because off to the pool we went. To my em-bear-ass-ment, the first thing the kid did was strip me down to nothing. My dignity was hanging out, not to mention a few more things, before *splash!* into the pool we went. Thank goodness I could float.

What I couldn't do was lather myself with sunscreen, which I needed because I was eventually rescued from the water by a parent, deserted on a lounge chair, and left to scorch in the hot desert sun. At least my nudity meant no tan lines.

Later on that night, a young man who was cleaning up the pool area from the afternoon party found my clothes for me, helped me get dressed, and carried me to the hotel security office. His hopes were that the kid would come back for me; my hopes were to never see the little bandit again.

Well, I spent the night in lockup. I was put to rest on a hard, white board and toe-tagged. I'm not sure whether I was pronounced dead, but there I lay. How was Paula ever going to believe my story? I believed I was going to be in some deep, deep trouble!

While I was wondering what type of trouble I was going to get into, Paula and Teresa returned to their hotel room. Within minutes, Paula noticed my absence and started hunting for me. She knew where I was supposed to be, and I somehow was not there. She and Teresa looked everywhere, retracing their steps from the front desk to the fifteenth floor. They had no idea whatsoever where I had disappeared to. From what I was told, Paula did not sleep well that night. How was she going to tell the children that Gear Bear was gone?

Come Tuesday morning, Paula and Teresa got up bright and early before their meetings and went downstairs to look for Gear Bear again. This time, Teresa suggested checking with hotel security.

Their first encounter with the security guard was astounding. "Ma'am, can you describe the bear? What was he wearing when you last saw him?" he inquired.

Paula responded, "He is about nine inches high, and he's wearing red shorts. He has brown eyes and a cute button nose."

Overhearing this question, my exact thought was, *This guy is as crazy as Paula.*

Well, Paula answered Deputy Dog's questions, but I believe Teresa was rolling on the floor, laughing and trying not to wet her pants. The officer said, "Just a moment," and walked back into lockup and brought me out on a white board with my toe tag still attached.

Paula then had to show identification, which the security guard took a copy of, before I was released back into her custody. As I was handed over, Paula was told that I was found in a lounge chair by the pool. She got half the truth but will probably never know what really happened. I knew what was probably going to happen: I'd be put in time-out for the rest of the trip—*as if it were my fault*!

As we were walking away, I heard the security guard say, "Ma'am, don't worry. My wife takes a pig with her everywhere she goes, too."

I wasn't really sure how to take that one. Was that supposed to be comforting?

Winning at Slot Machines
or Maybe Not!

Remember how I described my little brown peeps? Well, after a couple of hours of being in the casino with Paula one weekend, my little brown eyes were still rolling around and around in my head.

Seeing wasn't the only sense that was impaired. The bells, the dings, and the sirens were almost too much noise for my little ears. I imagined that pushing the play button constantly or pulling that long, black handle over and over and over could eventually cause some wear and tear on one's hand or shoulder.

I didn't even take into consideration that some people are marathon players and play a couple of machines at a time. One lady cordoned off two machines with a yellow cord so she could play them exclusively. I'm not sure if this was because she couldn't lose her money fast enough on one machine or if she just didn't want us sitting next to her.

With the whirling images, the noise, and the repetitive motions, I couldn't understand why a person would want to spend so much time sitting at a change machine. As far as I could tell, one could just go to the car wash and put money in the moneychanger. That would save that person a lot of time and money. The person would always break even and never lose money. At the car wash, a person also wouldn't hear the words I heard at the casino (that I probably shouldn't have)—words like "crap," "stud," and "poke her."

After doing some research and a little math, I have learned the odds of winning when playing a slot machine are 92.07 percent. So here is my advice for how to win at the slot machines: *don't play them!*

Da Bear Got Lucky in Vegas

This time I was glad I didn't follow my own advice about not playing slot machines. After previous Las Vegas experiences, in which I left all my hard-earned pennies there, I finally got lucky at a couple of slot machines at the Rio Casino and Resort.

Last night I lost my day's allotted allowance, but with today being a new day with new money set aside, I was ready. *Bring it on*, I thought

I started slowly with the roulette wheel. Now, I always bet on my family's birthdays, so after three wins and seven losses, I moved on, wishing my family members were born on luckier days.

Wanting to play something a little more one-on-one, I spied the Lucky Sevens machines and thought, *Those'll work*. Except right off the bat I could see a problem; getting up to the machine to be able to put my money into the slot to play would be a challenge. But did you know there are cute cocktail waitresses that are more than happy to help a guy out?

On the second pull of that one-arm bandit I hit a two-hundred-dollar winner. Another pull brought another two-hundred-dollar winner. I wondered if that old machine just thought I was going to sit there all day until my money ran out. Well, maybe I'd have one more try and *bingo!* Jackpot! Another winner, chicken dinner!

Not wanting to push my luck, I decided to cash in and return to my room and hold out until it was time to go home. I walked by another machine that looked good and thought, *Let's just try it once.*

Winner!

I decided I really needed to get up to the room before Leigh got upset and left for class without me, but there sat twenty-three slot machines and seven gaming tables between my Lucky Sevens machine and the elevator

Nope! You're wrong. I went upstairs with five payout vouchers and two twenty-five dollar chips.

See, I do have some will power!

Delayed Flight?

A delayed flight means *what*? On this particular day, I assumed that meant we didn't have to hurry to get to the airport or set the alarm for the middle of the night so we, as passengers, could be on time.

I do have to admit that sitting at an airport *is* entertaining. I witnessed a few people panic, not because of the flight delay, but because there weren't enough electrical outlets for them to plug into. As I looked around, I saw at least 90 percent of the passengers using laptops, cell phones, or iPads. I also happened to notice there were no televisions hanging from ceilings or pay phones or people reading books.

Who really needed a television when I saw one man nearly fall out of his seat after falling asleep? He rather resembled Elvis! Which might well have been true? After all, we were at the Las Vegas International Airport, *and* we did see Elvis, red scarf and all, on the strip last night in front of the Bellagio Fountains!

Having spotted a Bumblebee Transformer hanging out across the street, I could not help thinking the goings-on around me at this airport were pretty normal.

With all the nearby antics, a two-and-a-half-hour delay wasn't really that bad, as long as I didn't miss the bus to get back home!

Another announcement declared that we were delayed again, making it the fourth delay so far. Oh well, what was another twenty-five minutes in a Bear's life?

Besides, there was at least one good thing; Mrs. Lovely would not be on this flight!

Robbery in Progress

It was seven o'clock on a quiet Sunday morning as I rode into town in my usual cup-holder seat in the Big Girl Truck. Why would I be up so early on a holiday weekend? Well, I wasn't going to miss breakfast.

There was nothing unusual going on until I noticed Paula slow the vehicle as someone ran across the street in front of us. Watching out the front window, I didn't find the act of running strange, but the jogger's attire sure caught my eye. He wore a black hoodie that covered most of his face and bright blue latex gloves on his hands, which held a black backpack with camouflage trim. So this early morning athlete was either all scrubbed up for surgery, or he was an alleged robber who didn't want to leave fingerprints at a scene. I'm sure you guessed right; a 10-83 robbery was in progress.

The next question was whether we should report the crime or follow the suspect. *Of course* we followed him! What else would a good snoop bear do? Paula immediately turned right at the next corner and drove around the block to see where the person of interest was headed. We knew where he didn't go—anywhere in our sight. He vanished, obviously ducking into one of the homes within a short distance of the scene because the sidewalks, streets, and yards were empty. He must have had a well-conceived plan or an escape route waiting for him.

Now, Paula did give the suspicious person the benefit of the doubt, as she does most people, and thought maybe, just maybe, the person ran to the local gas station to pick up some milk while leaving a sleeping child at home. The child would be was why he was in hurry, except the bright blue gloves were a sure giveaway.

After looping around the block, we stopped at the gas station and discovered the door was locked and the woman inside was talking on the payphone. It didn't take long to figure out whom the woman was probably talking to. Within six minutes, three police cars appeared at the crime scene. Paula asked the officer if there had been a robbery. Of course, his answer was "yes." The police officer then asked Paula her name, address, and wanted to know what she had seen, including the direction the alleged bad boy ran.

Realizing I had seen a fleeing robber, I sure was glad shots had not been fired. I wouldn't have looked good with holes though me! I am also glad the slight delay didn't make me too late for breakfast. There is nothing worse than a hungry bear in the morning.

Having kept track of the story, I must report that no suspects were arrested. What I've always wondered was why would someone rob a gas station five minutes after the doors opened for business? Wouldn't there be a minimal amount of cash in the till? But apparently, the previous day's cash and checks had *not* been deposited in the bank the night before. They were in the gas station's *unlocked* safe.

With some time to reflect, old snoop bear here has come to believe the robbery could have been an inside job. Perhaps the cashier wasn't on the phone with the police, but with the robber, making sure he got away okay. After all, it was only her second week on the job! As I said, why would someone rob an establishment five minutes after it open compared to five minutes before it closed unless the person had inside information?

Oh, one more thing: No one, including me, knew the robber's race. I never thought about it until the police officer asked. Paula and I had no idea. We never really paid attention until we read in a newspaper article that the cashier said the suspect was wearing a mask. As I recall, the robber looked right at us as if he were afraid we were going to hit him. I wonder if his fright had anything to do with a fear that the Big Girl Truck was going to run him over?

'Twas the First Day of Shopping!

With doors locked and seat belts secured, off we went to the big city for the beginning of the dreaded Christmas shopping season. I cannot help wondering how many people buy a present for themselves in order to make the shopping experience more bearable.

The highlight of shopping this time was visiting the neatest store, Build-A-Bear Workshop. I always wondered how I came into this world. As I looked at all of the lifeless animals in the store, I was shocked. I never in my life would I have thought a bear hospital would be like that. Having been to Babyland General Hospital, better known as the Cabbage Patch Hospital in Cleveland, Georgia, I thought I understood where bears came from. Not even close.

It seems that in this "hospital," people actually pick the animal they want to adopt and then stuff a hose in its side and turn on a stuffing machine. With a little stuffing here and a tuck there, the animal is all set to go to the next step. What really made me cringe was when the woman took a needle and thread and started sewing my bear friends together. And that was *after* she inserted a heart! All I could say was *ouch*!

What was not painful was browsing through the astounding selections of clothing at Build-A-Bear Workshop. One could only imagine the outfits people came up with. It was like planning a red-carpet affair. I must admit I left with three new outfits and a gift certificate for a return trip.

The only problem we encountered was having a vehicle large enough to accommodate all the gifts we purchased.

It looked like it was going to be another good Christmas at our house!

Riding the Dessert Train

What more could a bear ask for besides a ride on a steam train? He could ask for a ride on a dessert train!

Our weekend adventure took us to the Boone & Scenic Valley Railroad and Museum in Boone, Iowa. Getting there involved a five-hour backseat ride for Ben and me, giving us enough time to ask "Are we there yet?" several times.

Wanting to be well rested when we reached the train station, we left Friday night and traveled about three hours west before stopping for the night. We arrived in Boone the next morning an hour before the first train departure time and had plenty of time to find a parking space, use the restrooms, and tour the James H. Andrew Railroad History Center.

Inside the center were lots of things for Ben and I to explore. I believe that Ben and I enjoyed the Thomas the Train play table the most. We got a chance to put our hands and paws on all the train tracks and cars.

We also explored the telegraph office and the post office. We saw lots of timetables and a bunch of uniforms that had been worn by railroad employees through the years. Because Ben set me on the floor, unattended, I was able to see all of the train lights on the shelves around the upper edges of the walls.

All aboard! Our first ride was on the Electric Trolley. It departed from the depot and traveled to downtown Boone and back. What made this trip so fun was that we could choose any seat we wanted, and on the return trip, we rode up front with the conductor.

Back at the depot, we just had a short wait before catching our second train, which traveled through the Des Moines River Valley.

Our assigned seats were at the rear of the train, so our view was spectacular. Seated at a table for four, we had plenty of room to stretch out. The table was covered with a white linen tablecloth— pretty fancy if you ask me.

As our journey continued west, we were served a light snack of grapes and cheeses and a beverage. As good as that was, the best part was yet to come—the dessert! It was scrumptious! But of course anything named cheesecake *with* chocolate on top couldn't taste bad or be unhealthy, right?

Along with the dessert, another awesome highlight of the train ride was passing over the Bass Point Creek High Bridge. At 156 feet, it is the tallest railroad bridge in the United States. Since the sun was shining, the engineer blew the train whistle several times, creating a beautiful rainbow over the bridge. It was a remarkable ride and a memorable day in the life of this bear.

Old Smoky

One of Paula's enduring memories that she talked about for many years was locating the whereabouts of Old Smoky, a locomotive from her childhood.

When Paula was a small child living in Milwaukee, her father took her and her brother fishing on Lake Michigan. Well, after the first five minutes, she wanted to move on to bigger and better things, like a Milwaukee Road steam engine named Old Smoky. At the time, the engine had been decommissioned and resided on one lonely stretch of track on Bay Street in Bay View. Paula said she always had a big smile whenever they drove around the bend in the road and saw all 412 tons of Old Smoky #265.

Originally, the engine operated between Milwaukee and Council Bluffs, Iowa, but by the early 1950s, steam engines were being replaced by diesel engines. In November 1956, a temporary track was laid and the retired engine was brought in, facing west. And that's how the story of Paula and the train began.

During the spring of 1957, the engine received the name Old Smoky thanks to a five-year-old contest winner. That year, Paula and her cousins took advantage of the fact that Old Smoky had not yet been fenced in and climbed all over the old engine to their hearts' content or until it was time to head back home. She passed many hours playing on that beloved train.

In later years, when the fishing poles and night crawlers appeared in her dad's hands she became sad, it appeared some engineering students vandalized Old Smoky by removing many gauges, wires, and other salvageable goods. Fortunately the vandals were caught and forced to restore the train back to its original condition.

On April 12, 1975, Old Smoky moved to Union, Illinois, to the Illinois Railway Museum. Talks are underway to bring him back home to Milwaukee. Wouldn't that be grand?

The Old Bowl

I'm really not old enough to be nostalgic, but I see a tear in Paula's eyes and a smile on her face whenever she brings out the old bowl her grandma used every Thanksgiving to make pies.

From what I understand, it was always Grandma's job to bring the pumpkin pies to the celebration. And of course, there was real whipping cream to top it off!

Paula said she remembered one time she had to use the hand mixer—not an electric one—and turn the little handle to beat the cream. Well, no one told her how long to beat the cream with the hand mixer. It became so thick Grandma thought she might have to put some yellow food coloring in it and use it as butter. Even now, Paula has no idea whether her grandma was being practical or just teasing, but every year, Paula seems to reflect on the memory of helping Grandma in the kitchen and "making butter."

The old brown bowl has been handed down for three generations, and we're hopeful it will last another three generations if not more. I understand the bowl was rather rare because it was made in the United States and because there is a stone around the top used to sharpen knives. I guess it is a multi-purpose bowl.

Well, the bowl served its purpose again this year and has been washed and placed, once again, on display on the cabinet to serve as a reminder of Thanksgiving pasts.

I am sure everyone reading this has experienced, from time to time, a memory or two spurred by a song, a smell, or even the sight of an old brown bowl.

Thank goodness we have our memories. Although we cannot live in the past, it sure is nice to be able to visit there once in awhile!

'Tis the Season

'Tis the season for decorating—*or* redecorating. For the life of me, I can't understand why Paula spent the entire day packing up the pictures on the walls and all the knickknacks, moving the plants around, and taking down the special don't-use towels.

At first I thought I should start packing *my* suitcase because I thought we were moving! Then a scary thought struck me; what if *I* was the next thing Paula was going to pack away?

What I soon learned was people decorate their homes in accordance with the season. With the Christmas season upon us, it sure seemed Paula was trying to keep up with the Joneses. We now have lights, bells, singing choir children, and even a few illuminated deer in the backyard. However, nothing tops my favorite decoration—the snow village.

Initially, I wasn't too fond of my place of honor on the mantle, but then I realized being on a hook five feet off the ground was the perfect location for me to watch Paula and the family as they built the latest version of the snow village.

Once in a while I climbed down to check out a new village piece, but, I quickly discovered I was a lot safer up on my perch. When I got down and tried helping as best I could, I became entangled in the holiday lights. Thinking I should play it safe and not get electrocuted, I returned to my spot and decided to supervise from above.

From what I could see up there, everything came together fine. We were ready for the holidays in no time at all.

Proper Attire Is Required

I just happened to overhear; honestly, I was not trying to eavesdrop on a young family discussing their previous night's sleep or lack thereof.

This was certainly not the first time I had heard parents complain about being unable to sleep after bringing home a new baby. What I listened to got me wondering; why do babies think mommy and daddy's bed is so much more comfortable than their own? I mean, parents go out of their way to make their kid's room just right. They provide matching baby blankets and curtains and all the stuffed animals possible to help the child feel safe at night. Yet the crowded adult bed remains a lure.

I can only imagine the thoughts going through a parent's head when he or she hears the pitter patter of those little feet coming down the hallway. I'm sure each parent is hoping the approaching little darling will pick the other parent's side of the bed to invade. *But wait, if there is already one child in mommy's arms, I guess it's daddy's turn.*

Allowing a child to sleep with his or her parents probably isn't all that bad, but for goodness sake, parents need to protect themselves. Mom, I'm sure you remember those tiny feet kicking inside you; now they're on the outside, and they haven't stopped kicking. Don't be afraid to sleep with your back away from those little karate kicking feet. Adding an extra pillow or two as a buffer zone won't hurt either.

Remember, even though the little munchkins used their uncanny night vision to maneuver their way from their rooms to your big comfy bed, they don't have a clue which way is which once they've been lifted into your warm little world. I have heard stories about parents having their noses and ribs broken from little feet in the wee hours of the night.

So the only other thing I can say on this subject is you have been warned! Use protection.

09/07/2008

A Stick Horse

Being a bear, I'm not too fussy about what kind of horse I'm riding as long as I'm securely fastened. After the faulty zip tie experience in Missouri, I was a bit worried about horseback riding. But I didn't want to hurt anyone's feelings by staying behind, so I decided to keep tagging along. I'm so glad I did because, if I hadn't, I would have missed one of the most enjoyable experiences in my short life—riding the great tundra of Alaska.

We were on a family vacation, traveling from Illinois to Alaska via Arizona. Yes, it seems like the long way around, but Paula is one who hates turning around if she has made a wrong turn. So after taking a left in Denver, we ended up in Phoenix, Arizona!

Again, getting there is half the fun!

Once we finally arrived in Alaska, we managed to find a small ranch of about ten thousand acres where the owner was willing to take us riding through the tundra and the area surrounding Denali National Park. After carefully choosing the correct wrangler to be our trail boss, we were on our way. Having seen several brown bears and their cubs while touring the park the previous day, I made doubly sure I was secured into my usual place on the saddle before departure.

During the ride, we didn't really have to worry much about runaway horses because I doubt they could run away if they wanted to. It appeared the Alaskan tundra, which translates to "treeless heights," kept the horses at a slow pace because their feet sunk six to eight inches into the ground with every step.

With one concern allayed, I focused on the wrangler and the rifle attached to his saddle. We asked him if the gun was for bears, and to my great relief, he replied, "No, the moose." In that part of the United States, moose are far more aggressive than bears.

The ride was unforgettable. But, of all the spectacular views I took in, the majesty of Mt. McKinley, the highest peak in the United States, proved to be the most breathtaking.

Although there weren't a lot of trees in the area we visited, there were a lot of thickets on the trails. Back at camp that night, I pulled a few thorns from my fur!

Because of this adventure, I can understand why Alaskan bears sleep all winter. With the roughly twenty-two hours of daylight during the summer, I imagine it's hard to get a decent night's sleep. Plus, they have a lot of eating to do. Come winter, the bears must be exhausted.

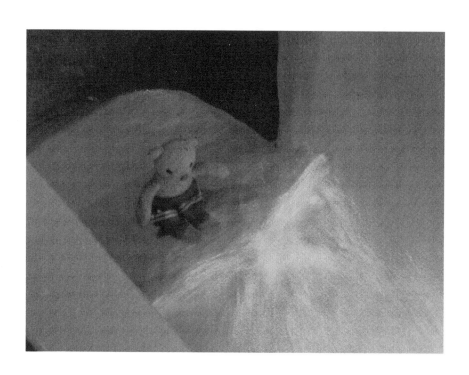

I Sure Spend a Lot of Time in the Water

How, in God's name, Leigh and Jana talked me into whitewater rafting, I'll never know. And I mention God's name because I was doing a lot of praying to the big guy that day.

Even thought I thought, *I'm going to die*, I wanted to be brave in front of the girls and agreed to board the raft. Despite wearing my own lifejacket, I made sure I was attached to the lifejacket Paula wore over top of her wetsuit. If we went overboard, I was pretty sure the guide was going to save her; after all, she was the one who paid for the adventure, and she would be the one forking over the tip for great service.

My security and confidence increased when, during the launch, I spotted two very young girls with their amputee father in the raft ahead of me. The presence of the girls made me believe the rafting had to be pretty safe. *If those kids can do it*, I told myself, *I can too!*

I wish I could say whitewater rafting was worse than awful, but it wasn't. Along with a few bumps, splashes, and close calls, I continually thought to myself—out loud of course—*I can't believe I'm rafting down the Snake River in Colorado. How cool is this?* Very cool, but would I do it again? Hell no!

When it comes to whitewater rafting, I can say I've been there, done that. I got the T-shirt and the photos to prove it!

Who's Afraid of Them Ghosts!

Usually, I'm the one involved in these types of stories, but on this occasion, I was just sitting back and minding my own business in my favorite spot on Paula's desk. Allow me to tell you a 100 percent true account about things that go bump in the night—and day.

It was nine thirty on a March Sunday when Paula parked in the garage attached to her office. Entering through the back door, she knew there would be no clients and dressed comfortably in black pants and a Wisconsin sweatshirt. Her plans were to catch up on a few returns and prepare herself for the coming week.

Walking to the front office, Paula stopped when she noticed two clay flowerpots and a wrought-iron basket lying unbroken on the bathroom floor. The pots and basket had been on the back of the stool for more than five years and had never fallen before.

As she picked up the flowerpots from their sides and placed them back in the wrought-iron basket, she figured a mouse must have run over the top of the tank and knocked the flowerpots to the floor. End of story and mystery solved?

About forty-five minutes later, Paula needed a bathroom break. She had not given the flowerpot situation another thought until, she saw something considerably stranger. The pots were back on the floor again. And again they were just lying on their sides, unbroken, on the hard ceramic tiles.

What were her thoughts? She increased the size of the rodent and believed the culprit must have been a rat. With panic setting in, she pulled out the rat poison and spread it throughout the storage closet, the bathroom, and the break area. She was very leery to even enter the storage room right next to the bathroom. Most things don't scare us, but mice—and bigger mice—and snakes are right up there with ghosts!

While watching Paula's hurried actions, I thought, *This chick must be one dumb blonde. Does she really believe a rat ran over the toilet tank not once, but twice in less than an hour?* And why wasn't she finding it strange that she didn't hear the pots fall when her desk and the bathroom are only twenty feet apart? The office was quiet—no radio or television. She should have heard something.

Satisfied that the poison was in place, Paula returned to her desk and concentrated on the fifty or so files she intended to complete. Forty-five minutes after sitting down, she was back up to wash her mug and brew a fresh pot of coffee. Because the only sink and faucet were in the restroom, she headed in there to rinse out her cup from the day before.

Start the eerie music! Yup, the pots were on the floor again, and Paula was instantly out the restroom door and on the phone with Patrick to ask if he believed in ghosts and if so would he please come into the office ASAP.

To his credit, Patrick arrived in six minutes, and after hearing Paula's tales about a so-called ghost, he kept his opinion about Paula having an overactive imagination to himself. Playing along, he picked up the unbroken pots, arranged them back in their basket, and placed them back on top of the stool where they belonged.

Paula was only a few steps away from her office when she noticed Patrick stepping out of the restroom, leaving the door wide open, and backing slowly toward the middle of the adjoining room. He leaned up against the post and thought, *Nothing is going to happen while I'm standing there.* But maybe two minutes later—right in front of his eyes—the pots came smashing down to the ground and broke into several pieces. Naturally, he yelled at the ghost, telling it to leave Paula alone and go away and that it was not welcome. He handled that a lot better than I thought he would; it did not faze him at all. He went in, picked up the broken pieces, and took them to the garage. That was it? Was the ghost going to leave because Patrick told it to? What power this man had!

Paula, on the other hand decided her work was done for that Sunday morning!

I'm ashamed to admit this, but Patrick and Paula, with me in tow, left the office for the day.

Paula decided that those files really weren't that important after all. She really didn't want to stay there alone, and what good was I? A nine-inch bear with no teeth and no fingers would be useless. I couldn't even dial the phone to call the Ghostbusters!

On Monday, everything was pretty quiet. Paula shared the goings-on in the office with Wilma. They both enjoyed quite the laugh. They would not be laughing long.

Tuesday was a somewhat different story. Although it was not as eventful as Sunday, someone or something continued lurking in the tax office. While Wilma and Paula were having their lunch in the break area, they both heard what sounded like a large bowl crashing to the floor in the hallway. When they went to investigate, they found nothing broken or out of place.

By the time Wednesday rolled around, Paula was okay with whatever was going on in the office since no one was being harmed. Her biggest gripe was the ghost did not seem to know the first rule of tax time: During tax time no one in the immediate family was allowed to die, have babies, go to the hospital, or take vacations.

Without going into too many details about what occurred Wednesday morning, Paula was seated in the restroom when her ponytail was tugged on. That was one of the fastest trips to the restroom I have seen anyone take in a long time. From that point on, Wilma started using the bathroom at the newspaper office next-door.

The following day at eight o'clock, Leigh and Ben stopped in the office before school because they were curious about what was going on in Nana's work bathroom. Well, as they walked past the bathroom and glanced inside, nothing was out of the ordinary—at least not until they reached the break room and turned around. All I heard was Ben saying, "I didn't do it Nana."

What was he denying? In the five seconds it took Leigh and Ben to walk to the break room and back, the bottom drawer of the small dresser in the bathroom opened and hot rollers spilled all over the floor. The two stared at the mess in disbelief.

On Friday evening, Patrick brought fish dinners into the office for Paula and him. As they were eating in the break room, Paula observed a white shadow passing behind Patrick's head toward the back door. Within three seconds, the shadow was gone, disappeared. She thought, *Maybe that was the last of the ghost; maybe it has left.*

Catching the strange look on Paula's face, Patrick sought an explanation and later agreed with Paula's assessment that the ghost was just passing through and hopefully leaving. I personally never thought a ghost would exit by way of a door, I kind of thought it would do something dramatic like exit through a wall.

On Saturday morning, a client arrived, and so did the unexplainable. As Paula went through the woman's tax return, she sought the normal background information and asked, "Do you still have all three children at home with you?"

The client gave her a funny look and responded, "No, I only have two children."

After a few more questions and some confusion on Paula's part, she searched the previous year's return and again found a third dependent, one with the name of Dylan. Now, the client assured Paula that *if* there were three children on her return, she would have noticed the error and brought it to Paula's attention since she took her tax return to the park district for pool passes.

There must have been an explanation for the discrepancy; the dependent's name was Dylan, and he was born in the year 1992, and he had a social security number, *and* he showed up in every return Paula had prepared for the client for the past several years. Okay, maybe there wasn't a good explanation, but Paula did send Dylan's listed social security number to the IRS to be checked.

The client only filed with two dependents, but three showed up on our software. So now the ghost must have been a computer geek too! Or maybe it was a way to communicate with us.

The client later provided some curious insight. Before revealing what she was about to tell, she mentioned that not even her parents knew the secret. She then confessed that in 1992 she gave birth to a baby boy whom she gave up for adoption. She did not know his name, where he went, or whether he was even alive.

Following the woman's visit, which made us name the ghost Dylan, the paranormal activities really calmed down for a while. Then one day I was sitting, listening to silence—my preferred sound—when the next client sat down for his appointment. Paula started the normal interview process with some small talk, asking Mr. Gary how his wife liked staying behind and working in the cold Midwest weather while he spent his winters in Florida. The man's answer was unbelievable. What Paula heard wasn't Mr. Gary's voice, but a very, very high-pitched woman's voice speaking her name. *"Paula."* I'm not sure if anything else was said because the response frightened Paula so much, she screamed and sent papers flying across the room. Her action started a chain reaction that scared the dickens out of poor Mr. Gary!

Keep in mind we weren't sharing what was happening in the tax office with too many people. Paula thought the fewer people who knew the details, the better it would be for business.

In a final plea to halt the activities of the unwanted guest, Paula hung a cross above the office door. Everything has been quiet ever since—except for one incident on April 17. On that day, while waiting for the water in her morning cup of hot chocolate to heat, Paula saw the boxing bag suddenly start to swing. Looking in the direction of the movement, all Paula did was smile and say, "Seriously?"

Paula and Patrick have two strong hunches about the out-of-the-blue haunting. First off, in late December, an antique jelly cupboard was brought into the office waiting room, so they believe the ghost may have been attached to it. Paula contacted the auction house where the cupboard was purchased but didn't receive any information on its provenance.

The next possible culprit for the strange activities could be a longtime employee and co-owner of the lumber company that used to occupy the building before the tax office moved there. Paula was told the man passed away the same week her visitor showed up.

I, Gear Bear, am not sure what to think. I just sit and watch the comings and goings that happen down the hall.

Road Trip Flush

Of course I want to go with you, Leigh. Are you nuts? Me passing up a road trip out west? You see, I have been tagging along with Leigh for some time now—usually to keep an eye on her for Paula. You know, to make sure she is safe and all.

Well, this particular trip was going to be Leigh's first trip out on her own. Even though she was twenty-three, which is pretty darn old if you ask me, I have had many more travel experiences in my short life. So together we believed we should not have a single problem. We were sure there was nothing to worry about, which was what she told her mother. A sixteen-hour drive and a one-night stay in a hotel—it would be a breeze.

Before leaving bright and early in the morning, we packed the white Honda with suitcases and a case of Mountain Dew. With the gas tank full and everything in working order, we were ready to head west.

The first eight hours seemed to take forever. We drove and drove and drove some more. Well, Leigh drove; I sat next to the shifter and helped with the directions and map reading. Unfortunately, I was not in charge of the radio because we have very different tastes in music. I wished I had packed a good set of headphones.

Our first stop was Lincoln, Nebraska. The hotel was quite nice, as was the front-desk attendant. She asked if we would like a room on the second floor, which confused Leigh. In her opinion, a room was a room. I knew what the woman was talking about as soon as she started explaining. She said it would be safer for a single woman traveling alone be on the second floor. Now, I am not sure whether the advice boosted my confidence in this hotel or not, but it sure sounded good.

Following a six o'clock wakeup call and a quick McDonald's breakfast, we were back on the road. Leigh seemed to be in an excellent mood for the early hour, but I guessed she was happy to be traveling on her own and heading to Colorado, her favorite place to visit.

What could possibly go wrong? Leigh did complain about the scenery though. She felt that Nebraska was a boring state to travel through. I just smiled and reminded her of the awesome rolling hills, canyons, and beautiful terrain just a short distance north of I-44. Every year I traveled to Callaway, Nebraska, for the River City Roundup Ride with Paula.

When we finally reached the *Welcome to Colorado* sign, I knew it wouldn't be long before we pulled into our final destination. We were about ninety miles east of Denver. Looking up at Leigh, I guess she read my mind. Rest area—potty break—probably the last one before Denver. After a quick stop, we would be right back on the road again, or so we thought.

Well, our little trip into the bathroom didn't turn out so well. The automatic-flush toilet Leigh used didn't flush, so she bent over to push the button, and that was when the trouble started. Her keys fell out of the front pocket of her hoodie sweatshirt and hit the water just as the toilet flushed. Down the drain went the keys. You know, the *keys* we needed to get back into the little white Honda out in the parking lot. The keys that were then going to start that little white Honda and let us complete our road trip.

Walking out to the parking lot, all we saw were rolling hills, an old windmill, and train tracks. Everything was as it was earlier, except we did not have keys. So everything was really different too.

"So," Leigh said, both laughing and crying at the same time, "what do you think we should do?"

There is always one thing to do when you don't know what to do—call Mom! There were two problems with this plan: Leigh's phone was in the car, and we learned one can't make a collect call from a payphone to a cell phone. After giving up on the payphone, we spotted a woman and asked if we could please use her cell phone, explaining whom we were calling and why we were calling. When Leigh got to the part about the toilet swallowing the keys, the woman started laughing, not knowing how a person could flush a set of keys down the toilet.

The woman, who was traveling with her truck-driver husband, proved to be very nice. The couple retrieved a wire hanger from their truck and worked for several minutes before getting the car door unlocked. Although we were inside the little white Honda, we still did not have a means of driving away since Leigh did not carry an extra set of keys.

While I waited around for the lock to be jimmied, I noticed Leigh's cell phone ringing. Now, I know for a fact my traveling companion asked Paula not to be calling every half hour to check on her, but mother's intuition must have spiked and known something was wrong because, when Leigh checked her phone later, the caller ID was *Mom*. As Leigh called back and told Paula our situation, she cried, sobbed, laughed, and then took her mom's advice and phoned the Automobile Club of Chicago.

Several hours passed before the tow truck arrived with a locksmith. The locksmith went immediately to work, but he was not able to make a new key for the little white Honda from the vehicle number. He then proceeded to remove the lock from the passenger side door to use as a mold for a new key. But the key did not work because the lock was too worn down. Thankfully, the locksmith was able to create a key from the trunk lock. After a few hours of sitting in the car with no heat, no battery charge left on Leigh's cell phone, and a set of parents worrying about us, we were able to start the little white Honda and continue our journey.

The next ninety miles were driven in peace and quiet. No music, no talking, no crying, no laughing—only happiness and a lesson learned.

When Leigh arrived home from the road trip, there was a gift waiting for her. Her father purchased her a tiny toilet that made a flushing noise when touched—just as a little reminder!

I'm Calling Shotgun

"You'd better pull over to the side of the road and do it quick." The order was not because I had to go to the restroom or because I was going to throw up. Nope, it was because Patrick, ol' Patty Perfect, was about to be ticketed for speeding, or so we thought.

We were on our return trip home from Fort Hood, Texas, having visited TJ for a few days on base. The trip was educational; we were allowed on post, and were able to visit the museums, and toured the areas where TJ worked and the barracks where he stayed. The previous year, we drove our RV down there and shared Thanksgiving dinner together as a family, in the motor home, out in the middle of nowhere, but still on base.

For our most recent trip, Patrick was driving, of course, and it was just the two of us cruising down the byway. We had just exited off the Oklahoma Turnpike when I noticed the red lights in my side mirror. My first thought was *car seat violation*. Although I was securely buckled in the front seat, I am not forty-eight inches tall, which meant I should have been in the back in a car seat. Most people might think this a little strange, what with me being a nine-inch bear and all, but this was how I always rode when Patty and I were traveling companions.

Well, we pulled over and up walked a member of the Oklahoma State Police. The officer asked to see Patrick's driver license, registration, and proof of insurance. The officer really never looked inside the SUV until he returned from his squad car. As old Mr. Smokey Bear bent down to take a quick peek in the vehicle, our eyes met. My fear must have shown all over my face because the nice officer paused for a second and then told Patrick, "You're free to go. I think you have enough of your own problems."

Savannah, Second Time Around

First stop: Charlotte, North Carolina. What better way to start the football season than at a tailgate party? It was the first game for the Carolina Panthers, and who else but the *Green Bay Packers* as their opponents. This was the first tailgate party yours truly had ever attended, and I must say it was pretty awesome. The football fans knew how to do it up right. Their equipment made them look like they were professional tailgaters. There were grills attached to bumper hitches, canopies, generators, blenders (for the margaritas, of course), open bars, and Wisconsin cheese. Would we expect anything less from Packer fans? I met alot of nice folks who seemed to be right at home with the food, drinks, and the all-around party atmosphere.

After a short walk to Bank of America Stadium and an even longer walk uphill to our end zone seats, we were ready for kickoff! Go Packers! It was only a little sad that the Panthers lost their first home game. Again, go Packers!

By the time we completed the l-o-n-g walk back to the truck, I was totally out of breath. We said goodbye to our old friends and best wishes to our new ones, and off we go, knowing we needed to head east to the ocean and then turn right to go south. We had been to the Savannah, Georgia, area a few years ago with friends from Fayetteville, North Carolina, but this time we were on our own. Because we were on our own, we took the scenic route.

Wilmington, North Carolina, was our first stop on our journey south. While there, we met Marvin Grant, a hammock maker. He was kind enough to take me under his wing and show me firsthand how his craft was done. He has been making rope hammocks for more than thirty-five years.

A lot about that little city was memorable, but what really stuck out in my mind was the trip Paula and I took to city hall. Wherever we go, it seems that when the expired tab on a meter pops up, the officer is standing right by the meter and we have to pay a fine. The store owner mentioned to us that he had seen the meter maid coming and went to "plug" the meter for us, but the meter maid turned out to be faster with her pencil than he was in locating the correct change.

Despite the parking ticket, Wilmington did not lose its charm, so we decided to spend some extra time there. Thinking that the best way to see everything in a short amount of time was to take a guided tour, we chose a horse-drawn carriage tour through the historic downtown. Arriving during break time for the horses, we treated ourselves to ice cream and wandered about. Browsing through the quaint shops was very interesting.

When the bell rang to signify the end of break time, we hurried back and climbed aboard the carriage. Narrated by well-established locals who definitely knew the history of the city, the hour tour was very informative. There have been several television shows filmed on these streets, which doesn't surprise me. The town's architecture was outstanding.

Our brush with the television world was having lunch at the favorite hangout for the casts of *One Tree Hill* and *Dawson's Creek*. The restaurant, Reel's, was located on Doc Street. My little mind can remember the street and restaurant name because Paula has a friend by the name of Doc Reel.

Down the road a few hundred miles was our next port of call: Charleston, South Carolina. They have open-air markets surrounded by many specialty shops. Paula purchased some of her favorite souvenirs at Custom Wood Gifts by Shelia. There she found small, three-dimensional wood pictures of local homes, businesses, and historical places. There were several shops offering these unique gifts.

In Charleston, we toured the city by way of four wheels rather than horsepower. We were always on the lookout for the best places to have lunch or dinner; we naturally asked the tour director to suggest several places. He failed to mention one of their local soups, She Crab Soup. It was to die for. Paula and I had never heard of it, let alone tasted it. Before leaving the restaurant, we made sure to secure the recipe from the server.

She Crab Soup was served at the next family night. It was rather expensive to make, but so worth it.

Years ago, the first time we visited, Savannah, Georgia, was unforgettable. We met up with our longtime friends, Gary and Lynn. Together we toured the city, visited the Riverfront, had a few sodas, ate dinner, and joined a ghost tour. However, most importantly, we had a chance to catch up on lost time.

Back then, on our last day there, while on a walking tour of the downtown area, we walked along a wooden walkway near a construction site. A wrecking ball came swinging down, missing Patrick's head by an inch or less, before slamming into a post that held up the walkway. We were so lucky he was walking at the pace he was.

Without any narrow escapes, our return visit to Savannah was much nicer. Like the previous time, we boarded a tour bus that took us throughout the historical district and near the riverfront district. One of the many places we visited was the Chippewa Square bus stop, which was made famous by the film *Forrest Gump*. The bus bench was relocated to the historic Savannah Theatre. We also saw the Mercer House from *Midnight in the Garden of Good and Evil*. At the conclusion of our tour, we definitely knew there was more to see in the city than we had time for. So again, we decided to spend another day.

It was dinnertime, and we decided to eat at the Moon River Brewing Company on Bay Street. There was nothing outstanding about the place; the food was okay, and the décor was similar to our brew houses back home.

However, what really stuck out was the after dinner stroll along the riverfront. While looking out over the water, I happened to notice an object floating down the river, and a dead body appeared before my eyes. It was a good thing the body was far enough offshore that I wasn't stupid enough to jump in, thinking I could save the poor soul. But, by the looks of the body, he must have been in the water a few days. Following a quick call to 911, the metro police were on their way, and we were out of there! Apparently, the body had to float down into the neutral waters that were under the jurisdiction of the Coast Guard before it could be brought ashore.

Our choice of hotels for the evening was the Best Western Savannah Historic District. Guess what street it was on? Bay Street. Let me tell you, several times throughout the night, I looked out the window and thought about the body floating with the current. How sad. Had we only gone with my second choice of restaurants, the Lady and Son's, we would have been away from the riverfront and having our dinner cooked by Paula Dean instead!

I'm not sure if I will be joining anyone on a third trip to Savannah. Seems that city has death, or near death, written all over it.

How Often Are We Short-Changed?

Excluding the incident, we had an awesome shopping trip to the famous Woodfield Mall in Schaumburg, Illinois.

Woodfield Mall is the largest shopping center in the state of Illinois and the tenth largest in the United States. Located about twenty-seven miles from the Chicago Loop, the mall attracts more than twenty-seven million visitors each year. Woodfield opened on September 9, 1971, with 59 stores and grew to 189 stores by 1973. There are currently 285 stores and restaurants.

I'm usually not a bear to complain, but I must air my grievance because I think what happened to us is a common problem, a trick frequently overlooked. As you may know from reading my stories, I sometimes mention the staff at a restaurant or hotel that went out of its way to be kind to a small bear and his family. I like to say something good about an establishment to help boost their business and to let my readers know of a special place they might want to visit on one of their adventures.

For lunch at Woodfield, we decided to dine at the Rainforest Café. Little Marie was amazed at the alligator pond and the animation of the gorillas and the dogs. Of course, the fish tanks also kept her riveted throughout lunch. The food and service were good, but not good enough to be shortchanged by twenty dollars. I started getting suspicious when it seemed to take our waiter about fifteen minutes to bring back the change from a $100 bill. Our lunch ticket was $39.99.

Paula found it odd that, when her change finally came, it included ten singles and a ten and a twenty-dollar bill. I assumed the server was thinking that, by bringing all of the singles, maybe we would not notice the incorrect change.

I have sometimes noticed that a waiter or waitress will intentionally make sure there are singles along with a five-dollar bill and the rest of the change. Is this so a proper tip can be left? Most of the time, I'm sure we receive the correct change. Unfortunately, that did not happen this time.

What was most upsetting was that when we summoned the waiter, even before Paula could finish the sentence about believing the change to be incorrect, the waiter had already reached into his pocket and pulled out an additional twenty-dollar bill. He then went on jabbering about how hard it was to find the proper change and that was why he had to give ten dollars back in singles. And how does that explain why our change was twenty dollars short?

The waiter's ploy normally might work because a lot of cash-paying customers automatically just pick up their change and put it in their pockets or billfolds and they don't give it another thought. I am also sure Paula would have done the same thing had she not found the ten singles in her change so odd.

Maybe the waiter really did make an honest mistake, but it did make me wonder how often this kind of mistake happens and how often a waitperson counts those extra tips at the end of the day from those cash sales.

Did we leave a tip? Yes, we did. Paula gave the young man the benefit of the doubt and assumed he accidentally shortchanged her.

Since this episode at the Rainforest Café, there have been a couple of similar situations, one when we were ordering from a KFC drive-through and the other in a book store. I am sure that both of these instances may have been an oversight, but overall, we really should be aware when we are paying and receiving our change. It just might be a coincidence that cashiers or waitpersons forget to give your change back. However, I really feel that makes or breaks a business.

Our Christmas Angel

Most people, I'm sure, think about their little angels during the Christmas season. I know Paula thanks God every day for the beautiful family she has been blessed with.

The timing could not have been better for me to write the last adventure in my journal. I was waiting for the family to arrive on Christmas morning. "Away in a Manger" was playing, and sometime during the night, Santa popped in and left lots of goodies and toys—probably too many! The presents were resting beneath the beautiful tree, but something was missing on top—the angel.

For several years, I had noticed the angel sitting off to the side. I know that Paula is very family oriented, so her thoughts were, *If the whole family is not together, the angel will sit off to the side. Only when everyone is present will the angel adorn the top of the tree.*

I also noticed there were several notes from all the past Christmases inside the angel. The notes detailed who was present Christmas morning, who was away in the military or in Mexico, and whose turn it was to place the angel on top of the tree. Again another year, and again another note!

The lovely angel has been with our family for forty-three years, and this was the fifth year in a row that the angel had not taken her place of honor atop the tree. Although she was not on her usual tree branch, I was sure the angel was still watching over the entire family, no matter where they were.

Merry Christmas to all.

Several people have asked about where the cover photo was taken for my first book.

The photograph was taken in Hawaii with Gates Island in the background. Like most things with Paula, there is a story behind the photograph, and in this case, the story involves what was behind me. See, she did not really want a photo of me. *No*, she wanted to document the nude sunbather behind me in order to prove to TJ that Hawaii wasn't just for old people. Since Paula did not feel comfortable photographing the naked person, she used me as a front. She snapped a couple of pictures of me, raised the camera over my head quickly, snapped another picture, and lowered the lens back to me.

I hope you have enjoyed my stories and our adventures.

Coming soon, *Gear Bear's Firehouse Adventures*

This will be my first children's book.

We have many more adventures to share with you in the coming months, and we hope you will be able to enjoy them too.

Gear Bear's European Adventures

Gear Bear's Mexico Adventures

Please follow me on Facebook and

www.gearbearadventures.blogspot.com

Edwards Brothers Malloy
Oxnard, CA USA
September 30, 2013